Pitching in for Eubie

By Jerdine Nolen

Illustrated by E. B. Lewis

Amistad
An Imprint of HarperCollinsPublishers

Amistad is an imprint of
HarperCollins Publishers.

Pitching in for Eubie
Text copyright © 2007 by Jerdine Nolen
Illustrations copyright © 2007 by E. B. Lewis
Manufactured in China.
All rights reserved. No part of this book may be used or reproduced
in any manner whatsoever without written permission except
in the case of brief quotations embodied in critical articles and reviews.
For information address HarperCollins Children's Books,
a division of HarperCollins Publishers,
10 East 53rd Street, New York, NY 10022.
www.harpercollinschildrens.com

Library of Congress Cataloging-in-Publication Data is available.
ISBN-13: 978-0-06-232580-8

Typography by Allison Limbacher
14 15 16 SCP 4 3 2 1 ❖ First Edition

In memory of my mother,
Eula Nell Nolen,
and my aunt Lillian Dixon
—J.N.

$\mathcal{A}$ big cloud of dust came winding down our road, like a tornado on wheels. *More mail?* I wondered. That was strange. We never got mail twice a day.

Mr. Weaver brought the letter right up onto the porch. "Special delivery," he said, handing it to Mama. "For Eubie."

Mama got so excited she rang the dinner bell. Jacob, Eubie, and Papa came running. They were probably scared to death. We only rang the bell at mealtime—or in an emergency.

Mama handed the envelope to Eubie, who took three long, deep breaths. Everyone got very quiet. Finally she opened it, cleared her throat, and began to read:

"Dear Miss Shorter..."

The first part of the letter was like a beautiful song.

"Congratulations! We are happy to welcome you into our freshman class. And, because of your impressive qualifications, we are offering you a four-year merit scholarship covering all academic expenses...."

"Mighty fine words," Papa said, clearing his throat. "Mighty fine!"

Eubie smiled. "There's more," she replied.

"However, you and your family will need to contribute $3,000 toward room and board for your freshman year...."

Eubie's voice trailed off.
I put my hand into Eubie's. Jacob reached for the letter.

Papa stopped the swing. Mama shook her head. "Where are we going to get that kind of money?" she asked. Then Papa stood up, hitched his thumbs into his back pockets, and paced back and forth across the porch.

Papa suddenly stopped. "We can do it!" he exclaimed. "We can raise that money if we all pitch in! We have the whole summer. After all," he added, putting his arms around Eubie, "dreams are meant to come true."

That evening after supper we made a list of things we could do to earn money. Papa would see if Ben Tilman still needed a hand. Mama would ask in town if she could take in sewing. Eubie would do more babysitting. Jacob already had a newspaper route, but he was going to check around for something else, too.

What could I do? I wanted to ask Papa. But I didn't.

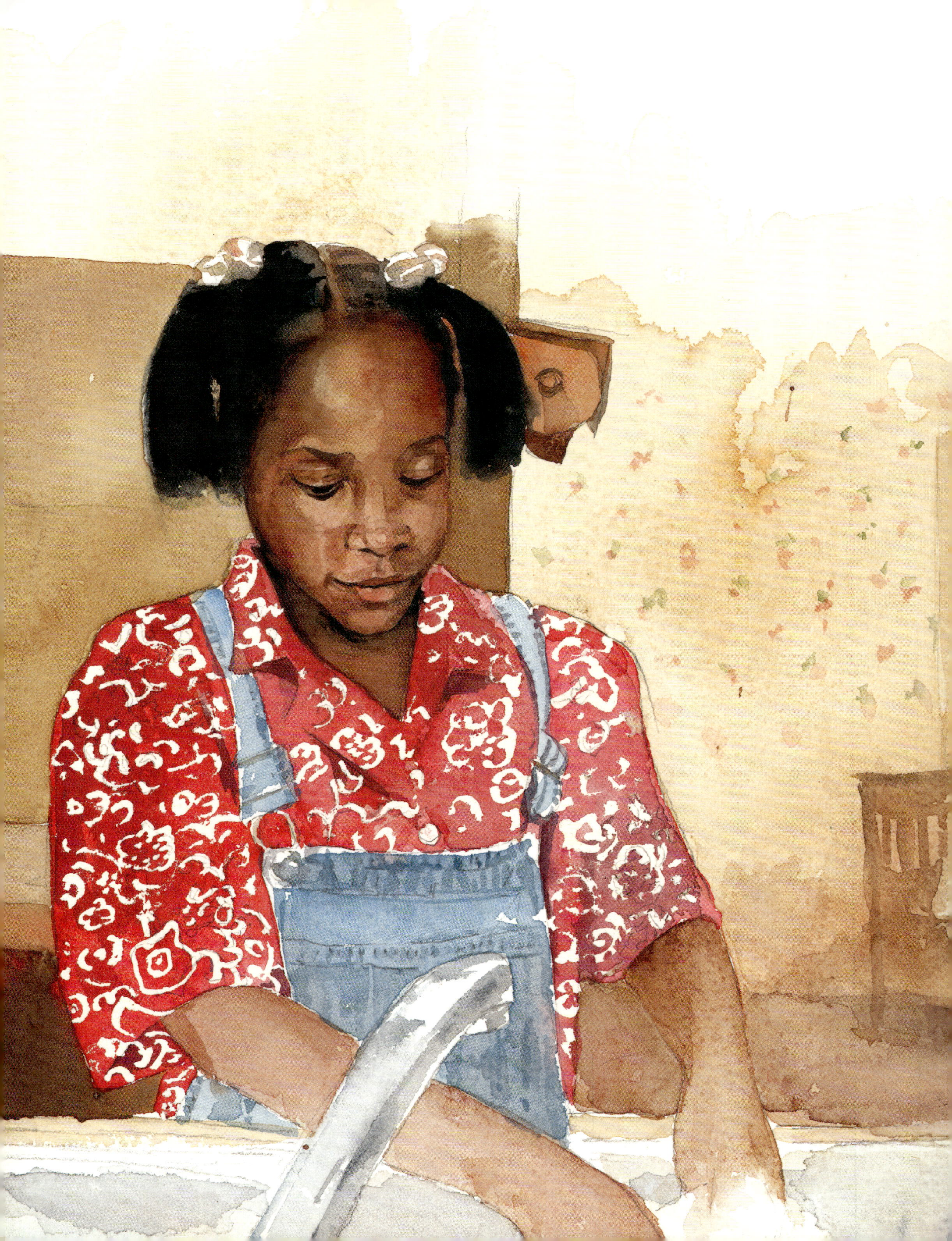

By the time I got up on Saturday, Papa had headed off to Mr. Tilman's. Eubie and Jacob had already left too. Mama was in the living room with Mrs. Tolliver. She'd come by with fabric and a pattern.

I ate quickly and started to wash the dishes. I knew Mama would need the table to lay out Mrs. Tolliver's dress.

The next day didn't seem like Sunday since Papa didn't go to church with us. He'd gone to finish up at Mr. Tilman's instead. While Mama sewed and I set the table, Eubie prepared the meal. Even as Jacob blessed the food, I couldn't believe we were having *leftovers* for Sunday dinner.

When Papa got home, he was tired. But I *had* to talk to him.
"I want to pitch in for Eubie too," I said. "What can I do?"

Papa took my hand. "You *are* pitching in, Lily," he said. "Mama says you're setting the table, washing the dishes, and feeding the chickens all by yourself, without even being told. That's pitching in."

But I always do those chores.

Eubie started working at Nelson's grocery store on Monday. Jacob got a part-time job at the gas station. Mama picked up Mrs. Malone's sewing. Papa worked in the fields.

And I finally got an idea. I'd put up an iced-tea stand! Folks needed a cold drink from time to time. I got a crate from the barn and set up my stand by the road. Then I waited for customers.

Jeb Foster's dog, Mouse, ran by chasing a butterfly. One of the cows leaned over the fence and mooed at me. Bees buzzed around the top of the iced-tea jar.

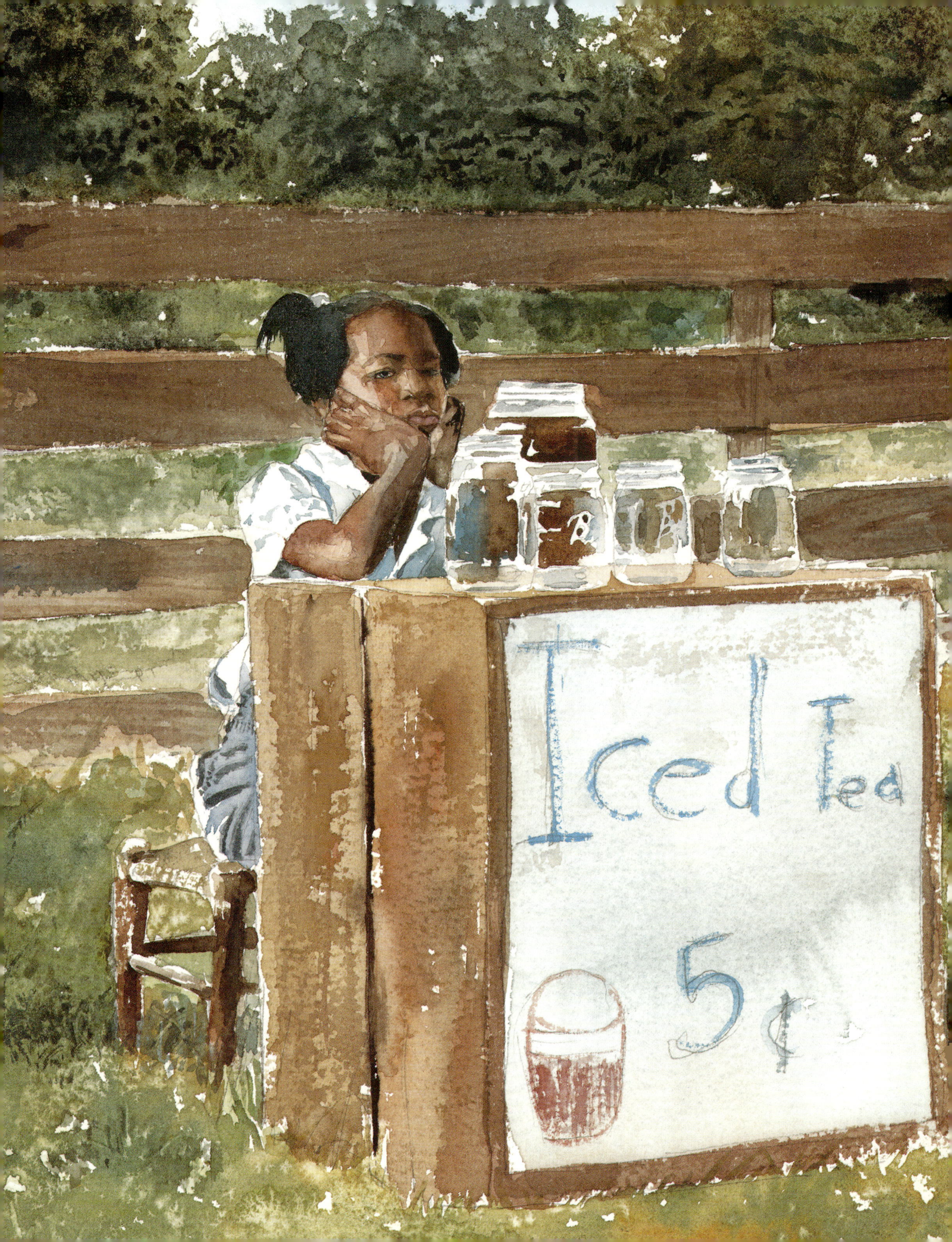
Iced Tea
5¢

But not a single person came by.

When the dinner bell rang, Eubie helped me put away the crate. I started to pour out the iced tea, but she stopped me. "Let's bring that in for dinner, Lily," she said, licking her lips. "You always make the best iced tea."

All week long everyone worked and worked. I set the table every day, but we hardly ever ate together anymore.

The next Saturday I sat in the yard digging for night crawlers. Lots of people went fishing on Sunday afternoons. So I thought I'd sell night crawlers after church! Eubie thought it was a great idea too. I put them in a box and set the box in the truck.

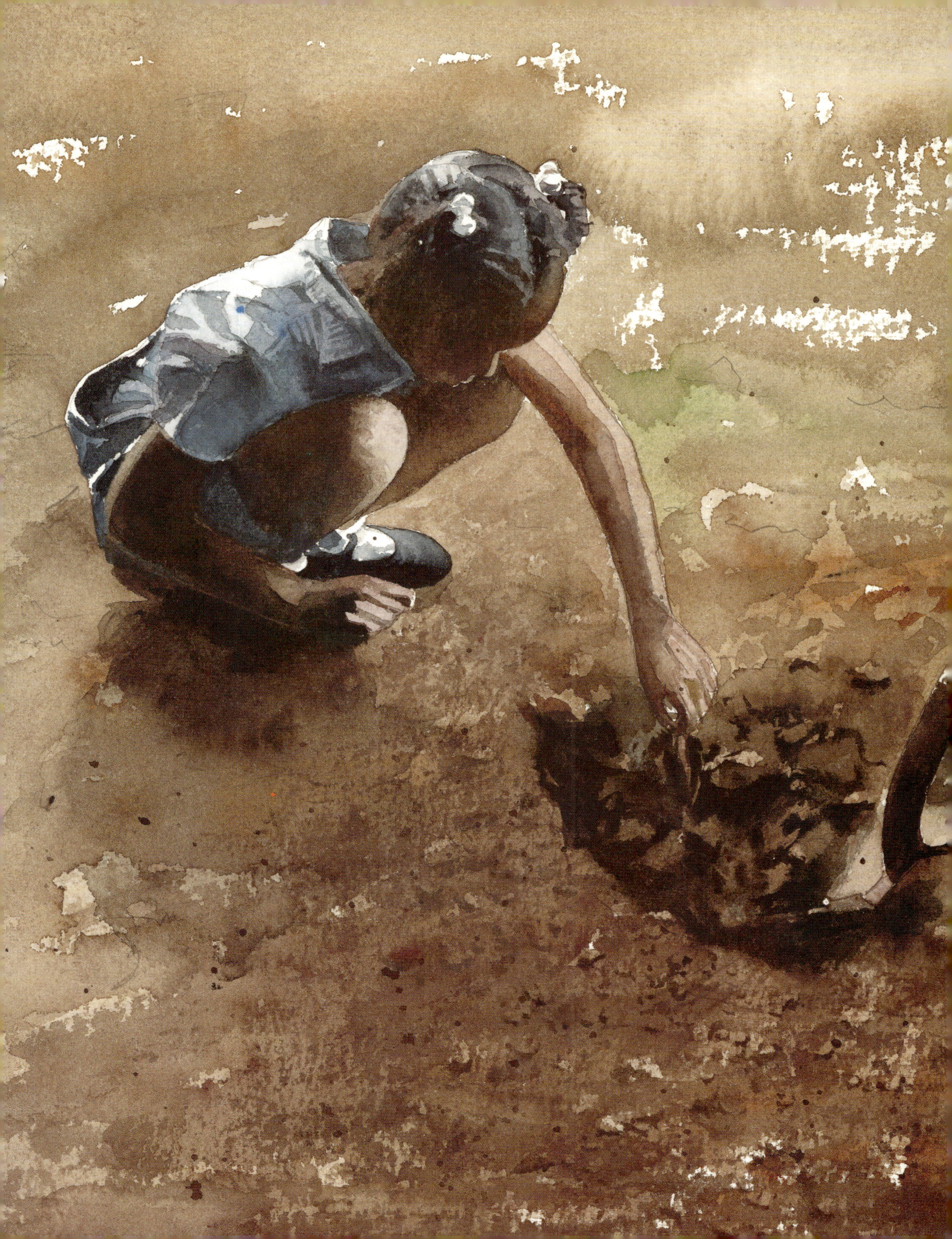

By Sunday after church, the night crawlers had all dried out. "You should've watered them or put more dirt in the box," Jacob said. So the next two Saturdays I did, but then it rained. Nobody wanted to go fishing anyway.

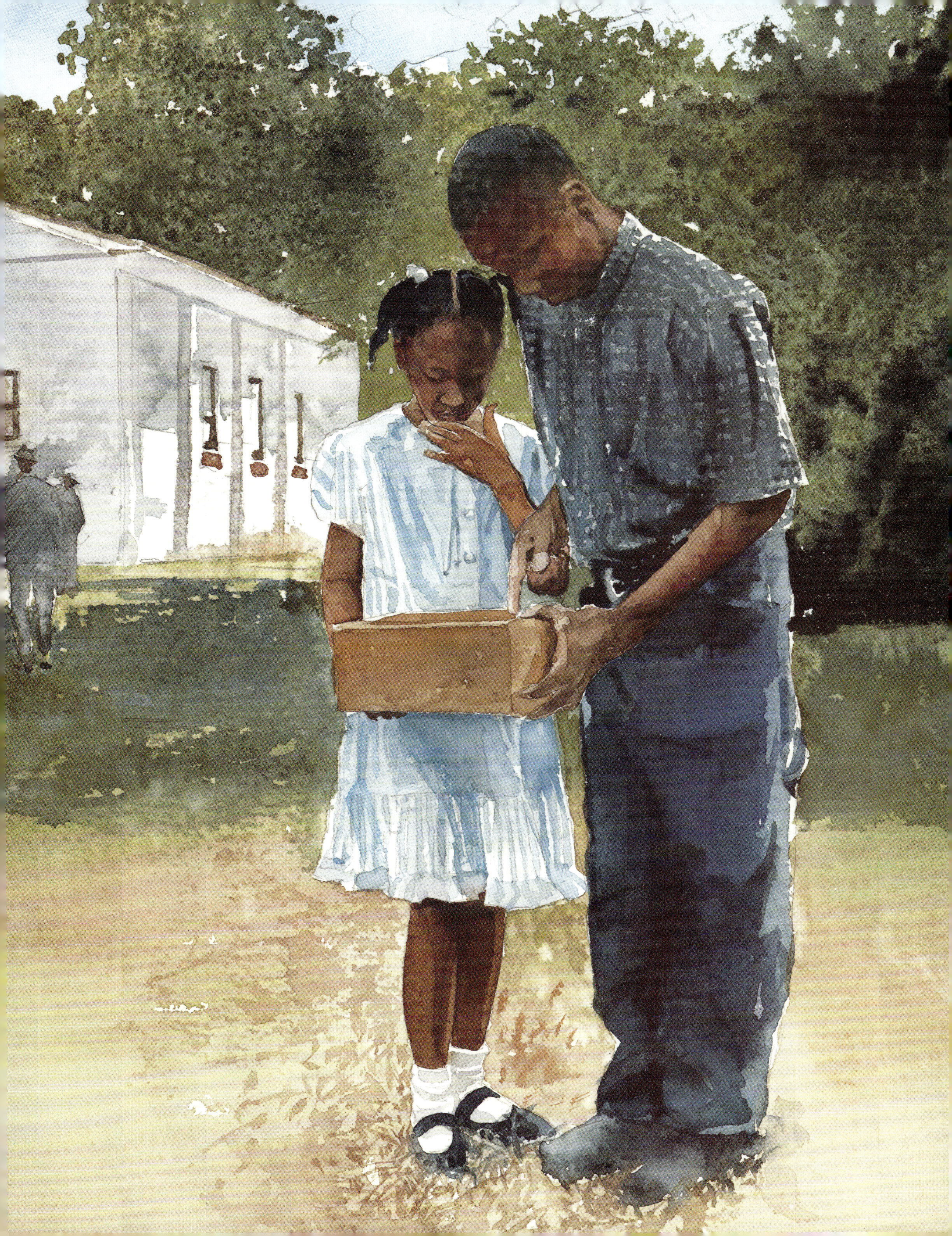

Three whole weeks wasted! It was already the end of June and I still hadn't really pitched in for Eubie.

That night I didn't even want to help count the money we had saved. I went out to the porch instead. There was stupid old Mouse chewing on a stick. As soon as he saw me, he picked up the stick and brought it to me to throw.

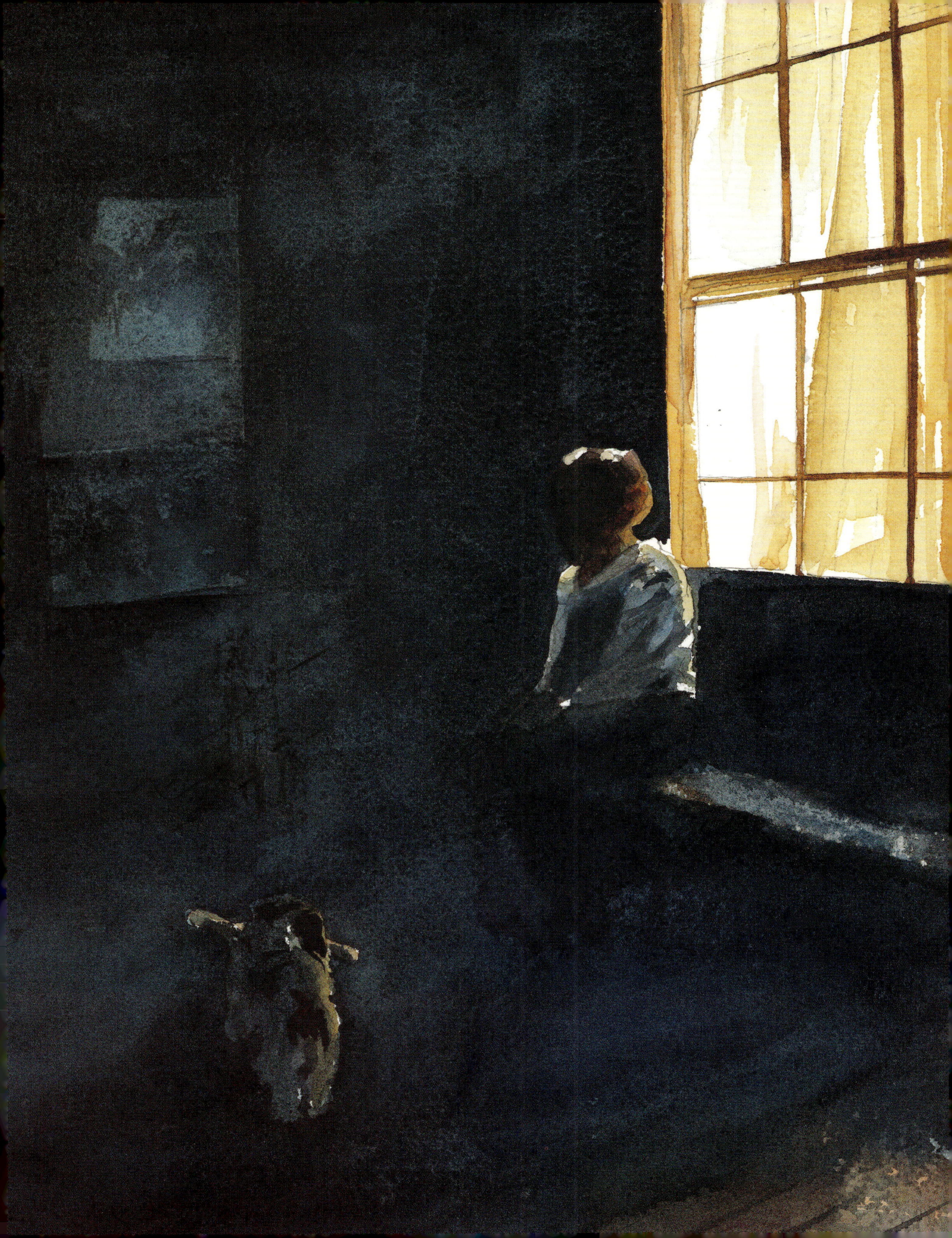

That's when I knew what I could do. I could start a pet-sitting business! I ran inside and got paper and crayons and started making signs right away.

Eubie and Jacob promised to hang my signs around town. I cleaned out the barn to make room for all the pets I'd be taking care of.

The whole rest of the week, I sat by the phone waiting for someone to call. I was still waiting on Friday when Mrs. Tolliver picked up the new dress Mama had made for her. It was for a wedding she was going to in Chicago.

"Fred and I will only be gone for two weeks," she told Mama, "but I'm worried about leaving Mother for so long. She can take care of herself all right, but she gets lonely."

I spoke right up. "I can help you out," I said. "I am very good at that sort of thing. I can look in on your mother and stay the whole day if she'd like me to. I could read to her. We could play games or go fishing. I can even make iced tea. And I can wash the dishes, too!"

Mrs. Tolliver laughed and then turned to Mama. "Do you think it would be all right?" Mama smiled and nodded.

"Well, Lily," Mrs. Tolliver said, "you do look *mighty* capable. And I'd be much obliged if you could help me out. I can pay you the going rate."

"The going rate?" I asked.

"Five dollars an hour," she said.

"Five *whole* dollars?" I couldn't believe it. "We have a deal!" I said, shaking her hand.

That night, for the first time in a long while, we all had dinner together. Eubie gave me a big hug. "Congratulations on your new job," she said.

"Lily spoke right up," Mama told everyone.

"Way to go!" said Jacob. Papa nodded proudly.

"I'm pitching in for Eubie," I announced to my family. "After all, dreams are meant to come true."

Not every religious leader was an enemy of Jesus.
Two of them showed respect for Jesus.
They placed his body in a tomb cut out of rock.
They closed the opening with a huge, heavy stone.
No one could get in. No one could get out.